ALL ABOUT BOND

Edited by Deborah Moore and Robin Morgan
Design Direction by Stephen Reid

First published in the United Kingdom in 2012 by:
Evans Mitchell Books
86 Gloucester Place
London
W1U 6HP
United Kingdom
www.embooks.co.uk

British Library Cataloguing in Publication Data
A CIP record of this book is available on request
from the British Library.

ISBN – 978-1-901268-57-7

Printed in United Kingdom

Evans Mitchell Books

CONTENTS

THE BOND VIVEUR
by Godfrey Smith

My most profitable meeting with Ian Fleming was in the corridors of The Sunday Times. I asked him if he'd sign the copy of his first novel, Casino Royale, which I'd just bought for 10/6. He was foreign manager and I was news editor. He cheerfully agreed and wrote in the front: "To Godfrey Smith, a fellow scrivener, Ian Fleming 1956."

He didn't say I was much cop as a scrivener, but never mind. Those nine words brought its present value up to £10,000.

To us young blokes on the paper then, he always seemed to have a mythological quality. We couldn't take him quite seriously, but you had to hand it to him: we envied his whopping salary – £5,000 a year, or some £200,000 in modern money. We called him Lady Rothermere's Fan; even though by now he'd made an honest woman of her, his legendary affair with Annie, the wife of the owner of the Daily Mail,

Bond author Ian Fleming chats with Sean Connery on location in Turkey during the filming of *From Russia With Love*.

was common knowledge.

We admired the lordly way he roared off in his Ford Thunderbird around lunch time on Friday to get in nine holes of golf before dinner while we soldiered on to the small hours of Sunday morning. He was the only man in the building who called our owner, Lord Kemsley, by his first name, Gomer, and Lady K by hers, Edith. We tried to emulate his principles: never use a subordinate clause and only call God and the King "sir". The paper did him proud in his 15 years with us: in return he gave us a sense of style, a baptism in dry martinis, a masterclass in irreverence, and a laugh a minute. He was good news.

I first met him in 1951, just before he married Annie and began to write Casino Royale. His fine Greco-Roman head with the nose famously broken by Henry Douglas-Home, the prime minister's brother, when they were playing the Eton wall game, came round the door of my little office on the executive floor. I was PA – then a job done almost entirely by men – to Lord Kemsley, or K as everyone called him, and one of my tasks was to

keep the key to K's private loo. Ian asked with a conspiratorial grin if he could borrow it. That was no problem, then or countless times later, because I knew about the mysterious role he played in K's life.

Robert Harling, our design consultant, who'd served with Ian in naval intelligence during the war, used to say K had six real sons (of whom one was killed in the war and another, Oswald, would die soon from drink), one technical son in C D Hamilton (later Sir Denis, editor-in-chief of The Sunday Times), and one emotional son in Ian. K had met Ian during the war at the Dorchester hotel, then a hotbed of (in Annie Fleming's words) "cabinet ministers, crooks and Mayfair remnants". It was supposed to be so well-built that it would withstand any German bomb. Among the flotsam and jetsam who had moved in there were Lord and Lady K, and they soon fell under the spell of the young naval commander with whom they played cards each night.

K was one of the three sons of a Merthyr Tydfil estate agent, all of whom were destined to become peers and

Ursula Andress in discussion over lunch with Ian Fleming on location in Jamaica for *Dr. No*.

millionaires. His older brother, Seymour, made his pile in iron and died young from a fall off his horse. Little is remembered of him, except the local joke that the good folk of Merthyr were collecting for a memorial – to the horse. But the £100 he lent his brilliant younger brother, William – the future Lord Camrose – enabled him to found Advertising World, a trade magazine. It prospered, and William sent for the youngest brother, Gomer, then an assistant in a Merthyr haberdasher's. They bought The Sunday Times for £75,000 in 1915, and by 1937 owned Britain's biggest collection of newspapers and magazines.

It made personal sense to split – Camrose had four sons who would want jobs to add to K's six – and was a politically adroit answer to the charge of monopoly. Camrose took The Daily Telegraph and the highly profitable Amalgamated Press. K took a ramshackle collection of provincial papers: the dim Daily Graphic and two failing downmarket Sundays, and would have left The Sunday Times with his brother had not Edith

pointed out that it would give him clout and reclame. From this it can be seen that whatever K's skill at sales and advertising, he was editorially naive and always would be. He was also a political innocent who made a ludicrous trip to parley with Hitler as late as July 1939 – and told him that one British politician he need not worry about was Winston Churchill.

So it is easy to understand how Ian would score a direct hit on K – and in particular on Lady K. Ian was the grandson of Robert Fleming, founder of the celebrated banking firm that still bears his name. His father, Valentine, had been killed in action in 1917 and was universally mourned. Churchill himself had spoken of his "lovable and charming" friend. Ian had twice been champion athlete at Eton, and though he had been obliged to drop out of Sandhurst after catching a dose of clap from a nightclub hostess, he had covered the Moscow show trial of Metrovick engineers for Reuters in 1935 and was now PA to the director of naval intelligence, Admiral Godfrey.

Ian's friends unkindly dubbed him "the chocolate sailor" because of his glamorous back-room job. In truth, he crisscrossed the world on His Majesty's Secret Service. He was twice at the wartime talks in Washington between Churchill and Roosevelt. He played a crucial role in what became the CIA. He flew to Lisbon and Colombo. He dreamt up ruses that were indistinguishable from later Bond adventures. One was to crash a captured bomber in the North Sea with German speakers in it dressed as Luftwaffe men. This would lure out the German air-sea rescue service, who would have on board a still-uncracked naval code. The rescuers would be shot and the code seized. Ian wanted to go in the bomber, but Godfrey judged him too valuable to lose. The scheme was aborted.

In 1945 Fleming took up his job as foreign manager of Kemsley Newspapers and began to assemble Mercury, a team of 88 men and women who were intended to supply the best foreign coverage in the business. A map behind his desk with coloured lights showed their disposition. The average age of the gallant 88 was 38, Ian proudly announced, and they spoke 3.1 languages apiece.

Above all, Ian was an ideas man. One day Annie received a letter from Somerset Maugham lamenting that he could not be in London for some months because he was at work on a book he had long contemplated: his account of the 10 best novels in the world, and why. Ian, who had long hero-worshipped Maugham, at once saw what a newspaper serial they would make. He rang Maugham, but the cynical old scrivener said he wasn't interested and no sum of money would induce him. Ian suggested the paper should buy him a small Renoir. Amused, Maugham still said no, but invited Ian to fly down to the Villa Mauresque. Ian returned with Maugham's consent to the deal. The fee was a modest £3,000 for up to six articles. Such was their success, the series was increased to an unprecedented 14 weeks and circulation rose by 50,000.

Ian showed his paces again by suggesting at another conference that we should commission essays on the seven deadly sins by seven of the most distinguished writers then at work. It says much for his acumen that six of his pairings went ahead: Angus Wilson on envy, Edith Sitwell on pride, Cyril Connolly on covetousness, Patrick Leigh Fermor on gluttony, Evelyn Waugh on sloth, Christopher Sykes on lust. He had suggested Malcolm Muggeridge for anger; in the end W H Auden proved an inspired choice. In a foreword to the subsequent paperback version, Ian suggested seven deadlier sins: avarice, cruelty, snobbery, hypocrisy, self-righteousness, moral cowardice and malice. Finally, he turned to his seven deadly virtues but in truth offered eight: frugality, charity, sociability, deference, sycophancy, neatness, cleanliness and chastity. The greatest of all sins he typically left to last, though it surely ranked with him first: being a bore. It was the only sin that never tempted him. Alas, they were never made into a series.

Surprisingly, Ian had always felt a failure. At Eton he was effortlessly upstaged by his elder brother, Peter, who sailed through the school picking up all the right accolades: captain of the Oppidans, a member of Pop (the boys' cabal that ran the place), editor of the school magazine. Ian had failed to get into the foreign office while Peter had got a first at Oxford. He had been dubbed the worst stockbroker in the world during his brief spell in the City (figures bored him stiff), and though he had done his country proud in the war, the sobriquet "chocolate sailor" still rankled. It was ludicrously unfair; Ian, far from choosing a cushy billet, had been headhunted by Admiral Godfrey four months before the war started. But still.

And then Peter had made an enviable name as the author of stylish, bestselling travel books. It was Peter who had described Long Island as "the American's idea of what God would have done with nature if he'd had the money". Nobody outside clubland had then ever heard of Ian. Nor did the Bond novels, when they began to flow from those two-month vacations at GoldenEye, his Jamaican Shangri-la, win many critical garlands. Annie confided to Evelyn Waugh that she was "scratching away with my paintbrush while Ian hammers away at his pornography".

There was, however, a new challenge that would enable Ian to demonstrate his remarkable sixth sense for the unexpected. He was offered the chance to write Atticus, then the only column in the slimline Sunday Times (it had just 10 pages when he joined us in 1945). It had been in the hands of some spellbinders in its time, but was now suffering from terminal hardening of the arteries. It specialised in paragraphs on what you call the younger son of a Marquis.

Ian made it crystal clear that he would brook no interference, even from K (who liked to print a grovelling encomium to each new Lord Mayor). It was a rum appointment, for he hated parties and loathed society. What interested him was how things worked. He had shown this predilection when, in 1936, he asked the bookseller Percy Muir to start collecting for him first editions of "books that had started something". That something might be as basic as the zip fastener or miner's lamp.

He gave Muir £250 to do it – not much even by 1930's standards. Muir entered into the spirit of things. For £4 he bought Marie Curie's doctoral thesis on the isolation of radium, Married Love by Marie Stopes for 15 shillings, the first rules of ping pong for free. Ian stored the books in posh buckram boxes embossed with the Fleming crest, but he never read them. He used to say airily after the war that the collection was worth £100,000; it was sold after he died to the University of Indiana. The same spirit of surprise, of being able to think round corners, made Atticus begin to get up and go. Invited to cover a world conference of top chefs in London, Ian did not fall into the trap of asking them how to make lobster thermidor or boeuf en croute. Instead he asked them how to make perfect scrambled eggs. They nearly came to blows as each argued excitedly for his own recipe and Ian got some sizzling copy.

He was lucky to have two young assistants who were both to become bestselling writers. John Pearson was 26 and describes himself then as "a humble hack". He had taken a double first at Cambridge but was still trying to find his true metier. Ian, he confesses, was "a dangerous role model. He was modest about his own talent but he made a marvellous Atticus". He gave a high-definition sketch of Ian in the authorised biography he wrote after his death: "the black hair greying now above the ears, the umpteenth Morland Special of the day already in the ebonite Dunhill folder, the lines of age just beginning to touch that sad, sensual, heavy-lidded face". The book was a smash. It enabled Pearson to buy a house in Italy, a flat in Rome and to become a full-time writer. He's published a life of James Bond, biographies of celebrated families like the Sitwells, Devonshires, and Spencers, studies of the star crossed gamblers Lucan, Goldsmith and Aspinall, and, in The Profession of Violence, a seminal study of the psychopathic Kray brothers.

The other young assistant was Susan Cooper, who had joined us straight after university. She now lives in America and is best known for her sequence of fantasy novels for young adults, The Dark is Rising (recently filmed), but has written many other books, a Broadway play and scripts for TV and cinema. "Dear God," she says, "it was 50 years ago, if I have that right, that Ian made it possible for you to take on Johnny P and me by offering to use us on Atticus half the time so that our salaries could be split. He was lovely to work for, appreciative, encouraging, patient. But if I wasn't talking about work I was completely tongue-tied in his presence: what with the height, the elegance, the cigarette holder, the curved mouth and the sexy, hooded eyes, he was the ultimate in sophistication to a pony-tailed 21-year-old from grammar school via Oxford. He gave me a lift in that black Thunderbird convertible once and I thought I'd died and gone to heaven, and was probably too nervous to utter a word all the way."

Not all women saw his charms. Liz Ray, wife of Cyril Ray, the man who Ian sent to Moscow as the only British correspondent in Stalinist Russia, said she'd only taken an instant dislike to one or two men in her life and one was Ian. Barbara Skelton, the second wife of our chief literary critic, Cyril Connolly, thought Ian's eyes were too close together – "and I don't fancy his raw-beef complexion". Cyril weighed in (rather ungratefully, since Ian had got him the job): "Very poor lover. Always gets up and goes home for breakfast." Rachel Terry, wife of our man in Germany, declined his invitation to go to bed but found him attractive. Blanche Blackwell, nee Lindo, a member of the Jewish Sephardic family who had prospered in Jamaica, thought at first he was the rudest man she had ever met; he was to become the greatest love of her life.

Annie summed him up best: "Ian was entirely egocentric. His aim as long as I knew him was to avoid the dull, the humdrum, the everyday demands of life that afflict ordinary people. He stood for working out a way of life that was not boring, and he went where that led him. It ended with Bond."

Then in summer 1959, K gave a twist to the plot worthy of Ian himself. He told his astounded directors that he was selling his business lock, stock and barrel. The buyer was a tubby little Canadian with pebble lenses who hardly anyone had heard of called Roy Thomson. K had quietly been buying shares in his own company to raise his holding from 30% to 42%. Roy paid £5 million for them. K knew predators were circling who might at any moment make a hostile takeover bid. He had recently come through a bruising strike with the print unions and did not relish another. Edith had undergone a disastrous facelift, which was to leave her with dreadful pain. The search for a cure consumed their remaining energies. His sons did not seem inclined to carry on. He died in Monte Carlo nine years later.

K had dropped one final clanger: he had pulled out of a bid for a commercial TV licence at the last minute. Not having what Thomson would memorably call a licence to print money was the coup de grace. Yet by luck or judgment, he had stumbled on two remarkable men in his time and given them their heads. One was Ian. The other was Denis Hamilton. He had entered the war with just three years as a junior reporter behind him, and ended it as an acting brigadier with a Distinguished Service Order. K had plucked him from the Newcastle office to which he'd returned in 1945, and brought him to London.

Five years later, he was group editorial director. He masterminded the purchase of Field Marshal Montgomery's memoirs and so added 100,000 to our sales. So K called him in and offered him a package to mark their years together. Hamilton opened it and found a copy of the cheque K had received for the business. He hung it in his loo and never saw him again. He and Ian remained close friends to the end.

Ian at once hit it off with Thomson and asked him for

a rise. Thomson refused, but instead offered him £1,000 a year to continue attending the Tuesday conference. This made sense; Ian's book sales were soaring, the film moguls were circling and the moralists mobilising: both Malcolm Muggeridge and Paul Johnson excoriated him for sex, sadism and snobbery. Their strictures read quaintly now when sex has become a national sport, torture is officially condoned, and celebrity has usurped snobbery. It didn't matter; Ian was his own man. And still the ideas flowed. He suggested that the story of how commercial TV was born would make a good read and I was deputed to write it. Ian was right: anyone who'd put £5,000 in ITV at the start found himself a millionaire.

It was Hamilton who suggested Ian's last big series: Thrilling Cities. Ian demurred: he was, he confessed, "the world's worst sightseer". He had often advocated roller skates at the doors of galleries and museums. Yet there were still one or two places he wanted to see. So he bought a round-the-world ticket for £803, drew £500 in travellers' cheques and set off for Hong Kong. Then he would visit Macao, Tokyo and Honolulu, returning via Los Angeles and Las Vegas. The most revealing point about his odyssey was the list of what he didn't want to see; in Tokyo it was "politicians, museums, temples, imperial palaces or Noh plays, let alone tea ceremonies". Instead, he asked to see a judo academy and a Japanese soothsayer. This unashamedly populist agenda set the tone, and its second European half: Hamburg, Berlin, Vienna, bland seeming Geneva – which he intended to open as if it were a tin of sardines then Naples and, finally, his old happy hunting ground, Monte Carlo. In vain did our editor complain that there was more to Hong Kong than pretty masseuses and whorehouses; what about the million unemployed? The world read on, as it has ever since the electrifying opening sentence of Casino Royale: "The scent and smoke and sweat of a casino are nauseating at three in the morning."

One question perennially fascinates Ian's legion of aficionados: how much of him was there in Bond? The answer, surely, is that though they overlapped in scores of ways – cars, caviar, sun, sea, gadgets, girls – Bond was still a fantasy; a projection of the man Ian could never quite be. When Bond, we learn on page 007 (of all pages) in Casino Royale, goes to sleep, his face becomes a taciturn mask – "cynical, brutal, cold". That does not sound at all like the real Ian, who found the only street violence he ever encountered – in Istanbul – distinctly upsetting; who drove his vintage Bentley tidily but never recklessly, and who swam well away from the sharks when he was at GoldenEye.

It doesn't sound like the Ian who sat down and wrote a personal letter to each member of his (by now much-diminished) staff when he finally resigned, and did his best to see they all had jobs. Nor does it sound at all like the Ian who wandered into the next room when Annie was having their only son, Caspar, in the Lindo Wing of St Mary's Hospital, buried his face in the lap of the woman in it who'd just had her baby, and wept because his wife was having such a terrible time. Her name, it so happens, was Moira Shearer, the ballerina and wife of Ludovic Kennedy: "Suddenly he got up, took my hand, kissed it and said, 'You've been such a help.' I never saw him again."

I remember him once telling me that Sophia Loren had been on the set of one of her films in Italy, and the technicians had called down from their hoists that they'd like to give her a saliva pyjama. "They meant they wanted to lick her all over," he added helpfully, in case I didn't understand. Dear Ian. "I know he's a child but I love him," said Annie. She wasn't the only one ∎

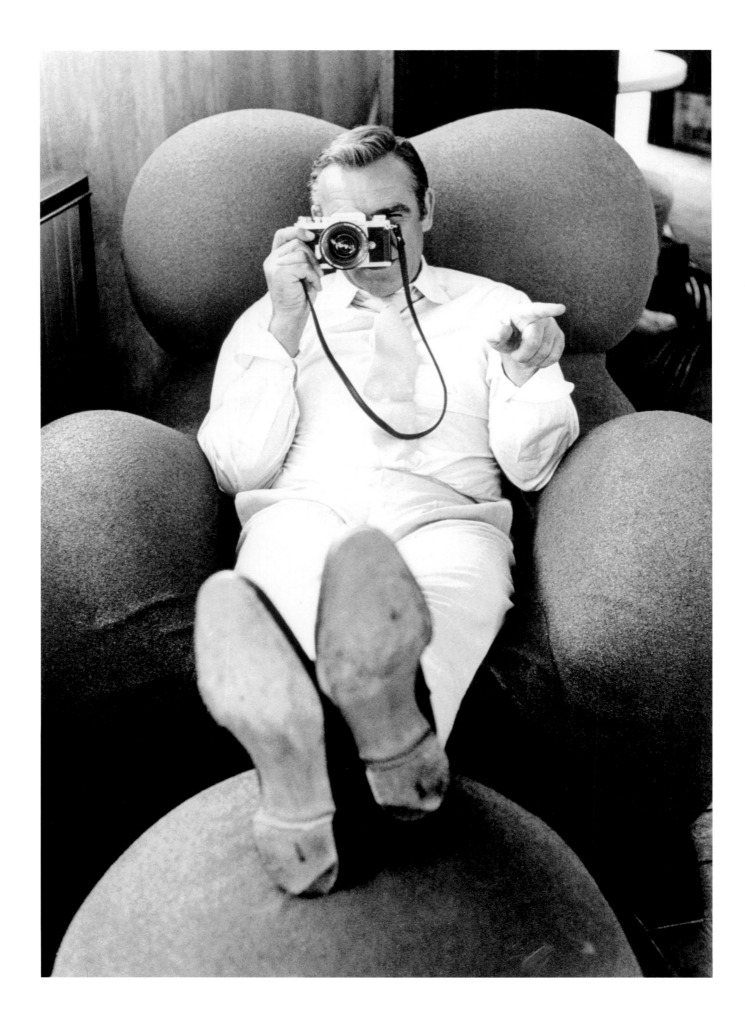

SEAN CONNERY
by George Perry

He may have defined the screen persona of James Bond, but Sean Connery was not the first choice. Or even for that matter, the second, or third. Ian Fleming wanted someone much smoother and classier, a public-school action man with a caddish, ruthless streak, someone like David Niven who was his preference. Harry Saltzman and Cubby Broccoli initially hankered after Cary Grant, so impressive in *North by Northwest*, then seriously considered James Mason, Patrick Mc-Goohan, Trevor Howard, Christopher Lee, and even Rex Harrison (a spy in a 1940 Carol Reed film) before settling on the relatively unknown Scot. They experienced the energy Connery generated as soon as he entered the room. Broccoli's wife Dana, clinched it when she confirmed that the rugged Scotsman's sexual aura was catnip to women. Fleming, although initially sceptical, was sufficiently reconciled to his performance in *Dr. No*, which had been carefully moulded by its director Terence Young, that in the next book, You Only Live Twice he would modify 007's character to give him some Scottish antecedents and an improved sense of humour. Not long afterwards the author died, but by then well aware that his literary creation had spawned a British superstar.

Unlike Fleming and Bond, Connery's background was far from Eton. A Scot, with Irish antecedents, he was born in 1930, and raised in the rough Fountainbridge neighbourhood of Edinburgh. He left school to become a Co-op milkman, delivering bottles from a horse-drawn cart for a pound a week. His national service in the navy ended with a duodenal ulcer, and he went back to the milk round for a while before drifting into a multiplicity of jobs that included truck-driving, polishing coffins, and spells as a welterweight boxer and modelling for a life class. His well-developed, muscular 6 ft 2 in physique led him into body-building, even to entering Mr Universe competitions and picking up a prize or two. He considered a career in professional football, but was lured instead to the stage, securing a chorus role as a beefy sailor in the touring cast of South Pacific.

There was nothing overnight about his acting ascent. He slogged away for years, making his film debut in a near-invisible walk-on moment in *Lilacs In The Spring* (1955). At first he made a better living posing in swimwear for Vince's Manshop. Meanwhile he was applying himself assiduously in filling the gaps from an inadequate education. He embarked on a phenomenal reading programme that embraced the classics, science and discovery, philosophy and great literature, turning himself into something of an auto-didact. Many have rued their error in underestimating the breadth of his knowledge.

The film parts began trickling in. A gangster in *No Road Back*, a trucker in *Hell Drivers*, a welder in *Time Lock*, a first-time appearance for Terence Young in an action thriller *Action Of The Tiger* (all 1957). He then played the leg of a triangle with Lana Turner in *Another Time, Another Place* (1958), and gained press attention

15

when her hoodlum lover Johnny Stompanato stormed the set brandishing a gun, accusing Connery of having an affair with her. Watched admiringly, Connery swiftly decked and disarmed him. Then came a lead part in an engaging Irish whimsy for Disney, *Darby O'Gill And The Little People* (1959) in which he actually sang, and it was that performance that caught the eye of Cubby Broccoli.

From the moment he uttered the words "Bond. James Bond" Connery established the screen persona ensuring that it would become a series, although nobody in 1962 imagined it still continuing half-a-century later. Connery clicked as Bond precisely because he was not the standard, stiff-upper-lip British hero type with a superior accent. Rarely has he disguised his agreeable Scottish brogue with its hissing sibilants, be it as Bond, or a Soviet submarine commander or a Chicago cop. In the later Bond films from *Goldfinger* on, Connery's hair was thinning so fast that he had to wear a toupee.

Bond was the platform that turned Sean Connery into the biggest-ever British star attaining the magic level of bankability respected by Hollywood. He played his game shrewdly. While performing Bond he was always aware that it was not a career in itself, and appeared in other films such as Hitchcock's *Marnie* (1964) and Sidney Lumet's *The Hill* (1965). He even quit Bond after half-a-dozen appearances, claiming he was under-remunerated, but was persuaded back for *Diamonds Are Forever* (1971) for which he was paid $1.25 million. That was his last official Bond film, but in 1983 he returned for *Never Say Never Again*, which was outside the regular franchise, and was almost in direct competition with Roger Moore in *Octopussy*. Connery earned $6.4 million, but although the film was financially successful it ended slightly behind its rival.

He has a reputation for prickliness, and a litigious streak. In 1965 he upset feminists with a Playboy interview in which he asserted that it was all right to hit women when they deserved it. His first marriage, the actress Diane Cilento in 1962 ended unhappily, but since

Sean Connery clown's for Terry's camera on the set of *Goldfinger* (1964) at Pinewood Studios.

1975 he has been firmly wedded to the French painter Micheline Rocquebrune. For many years they lived in a villa overlooking the Mediterranean at Marbella, adjacent to a golf course where he could engage his passion, but eventually left after his disenchantment with the Spaniards, and relocated to the Bahamas.

At his career height he would travel light, with just a carry-on bag. Certain hotels in New York, London, Paris and elsewhere had closets in which he maintained a full set of clothes and accessories. "Why pay excess baggage charges?" On the many occasions when I have met him, both domestically and in a work context, I have always been impressed by his serious approach. He is surprisingly straightforward in a business where insincerity is the default mode, and speaks his mind, not without humour. On set he expects everyone to strive for a level of professionalism equal to his own. I once saw him purple with rage at *Cinecittà* because Italian-made films use looped dialogue, rather than direct recording. The order "Silenzio!" before a take is regarded as only advisory, and technicians go on chatting while the actors are trying to do their stuff. Not with Connery around.

His career extended far beyond 007. He won an Oscar for *The Untouchables*, a Bafta for *The Name Of The Rose*. His presence was usually enough to give a film distinction, and top directors he worked with included Huston, Boorman, Gilliam, De Palma, Van Sant and Spielberg. The Queen knighted him in 2000. Previous attempts to secure the accolade had foundered because of his fervent Scottish nationalism. He acquired tattoos on his arm in the navy, long before such embellishments became chic. One says "Mum and Dad", the other "Scotland Forever". Even though he has been designated as "the greatest living Scot" he has sometimes attracted disapproval from his countrymen because he refuses to live there, preferring warmer climes. It is a trifle. After all, he has only done what a Scotsman does best, and that is to go out into the wide world and give it a good kicking ■

Even a Bond film set has long periods of tedious downtime waiting for the cameras to roll. During filming of *Diamonds Are Forever* in 1971 the photographer Terry O'Neill caught him cat-napping. "He had a fight scene to film with two girls called Bambi & Thumper (played by Lola Larson & Trina Parks) but he'd been out partying in Vegas the night before."

Sean Connery queues for his lunch along with members of the crew, including director Guy Hamilton (in hat) and screenwriter Tom Mankiewicz (in checked trousers). Right: Sean Connery was persuaded by O'Neill to practise a few shots on the Hollywood 'moon set' in homage to astronaut Alan Shepard's famous Apollo 14 mission in 1971 when he took a six iron and balls to the moon.

Connery had a reputation for being a serious and demanding workaholic but, remembers O'Neill, "he loved his golf, he wasn't afraid to muck about and he had a wicked sense of humour. It wasn't all work hard, play hard – he was a working class lad and he was easy going around the crew."

In those days (1971),
photographers were every bit
as important as cast and crew
– their stills provided the publicity
that meant the difference
between box office success and
failure. "It meant I could shoot
candid and private moments
(above, right and over-page)
non-stop without being
controlled or manipulated by
movie executives or stars'
management, as photographers
are today," says O'Neill.

Filming on Ken Adam's sets for *Diamonds Are Forever* at Pinewood Studios.

PAUL BAXLEY
1902 1970

Sean photographed on location at a crematorium on the outskirts of Las Vegas. As an in-joke
the crew fashioned the deceased's nameplate to feature US Stunt Arranger Paul Baxley's name.

On location for *Diamonds Are Forever* at Kirk Douglas' house in Palm Springs. "Jill St John was a great Bond girl. She wasn't just a pretty face with a great body, she had a good brain and she hit it off with Sean straight away," recalls O'Neill. "She was vivacious and as Tiffany Case, the first real female character to compete with Bond on screen."

"In between takes, Sean
loved to wander down to the
casino floor and have a little
flutter on the slots. It wasn't
just about killing time.
Naturally I went with him."

Sean in Vegas. "Sean and
I took a little trip back
stage between takes and
the showgirls all wanted to
be photographed with
James Bond," says O'Neill.

Bond is left holding Plenty O'Toole's dress while she visits the bathroom (right). Above, In a scene that was cut from the release print of *Diamonds Are Forever*, James Bond treats Plenty O'Toole to dinner.

PUSSY GALORE
by Honor Blackman

"Pussy Galore was a feminist, though you didn't know by the end of the film that she was a feminist, once she had succumbed to Bond's charm. She changed sides, from the wicked man to the good. As a viewer, you know that somebody who can have their own air force and fly a plane is rather special. Especially then. She was a great character to play. That's why I get fed up when people call us 'Bond girls'. Some of them certainly were – they'd take one look at Bond and fall flat on their backs – but Pussy Galore wasn't one of those.

She put up a fight. I don't know why she bothered. Sean is the sexiest man, probably, I have ever met. Because he had everything, didn't he, including that ridiculous accent. He was fun. He was very professional, but he was easy to work with. We worked that scene out very carefully beforehand. They are not keen that you should have to do it twice, because they are afraid you might not live to do the next one. It was the way you do stunts, you work out exactly beforehand how they are supposed to go.

The lighting cameraman was such a lovely fellow – Ted Moore – and he asked us if we would mind lying in the hay while he lit it, because it was such a tight close-up that he didn't want to put the stand-ins in. Ted wanted to set fire to the hay, I think. It's a great scene. Everything I did was at Pinewood, apart from one shot at Northolt airport. I never went anywhere exotic… never!

I was aware that the name Pussy Galore was very contentious and when I went to the States that was very obvious. Some of the presenters couldn't say it, and some of them asked, how could I play such a part? To take it so seriously seemed to me ridiculous. And if you read Fleming, you know that it reflects the character. Oddjob, Goldfinger, all that. Well, if you've that kind of mind, then worry about it. As far as I was concerned, it didn't bother me.

I don't know why the character is so loved. I suppose it was obvious there was great chemistry. And it's a good story. We had the advantage, at the beginning, because we had all the best Fleming stories. There was *Dr. No* and *From Russia With Love* and then we were the third. As time went on, the stories were less and less good. They relied on more and more gadgets. But ours were the best stories. And with my wicked name, and Goldfinger, who was so well-played, and Oddjob, who caught everyone's imagination – I'm not surprised it's so popular.

Looking back, I think what I did was extraordinary. For that scene in *Goldfinger* they put down so much hay for me to land on, and said, 'Is this alright?' Well, I'd just been doing it on cement for two years, with *The Avengers*, so it was an absolute piece of cake as far as I was concerned. Nobody would do it now. I've often thought that I must have been potty and they must have been very surprised that I was so game.

I knew nothing about judo when I started *The Avengers*. It wasn't till, I think, about the third episode, when I got fed up with the scripts saying, 'Cathy reach-

es into the bag for her gun' – because every female knows, we'd be dead as dodos by the time you found it – that I asked if I could have a go. There was a fellow in the cast who'd taken some classes, and he showed me a simple throw which I did with such aplomb – being a girl, you have to do it right – and they all thought it was terribly exciting and off I was posted to my lessons. I thought I'd have private lessons, but I was on all the sweaty mats with the sweaty chaps… ugh!

I got to brown belt. It was ridiculous the way I had to learn, in such a short time, jumping here and going back. I mean, stomach throws. God knows, it takes some time to get to those. You grab him by the lapels, you put your foot in his chest, and then you throw him backwards over your head. Every week they gave me a bigger and better man. If you didn't do it right, he fell on your face, which wasn't very funny, so you made absolutely sure you gave a good kick. But, you know, you'd go right onto the cement, because you drop onto your bottom. And because I've got hardly any bottom,

you go right onto the base of your spine and you've got this great weight coming over you. I must have been out of my mind.

It did feel empowering, and of course the females of the country all went mad because they thought, at last! Men are so bloody superior and now they aren't, any more. I don't think my friends were surprised, because it's me. My mother always worried as to whether I should get hurt. Sadly my father was no longer with us then – he would have loved it. My mother was not a physically strong woman, on the contrary. She lived to 92 although she had all the chest problems I've inherited, but she wasn't a bit butch, at all.

Everybody was staggered that I left *The Avengers*. We were on tape, in black and white, with piss-poor money, and we were just going onto colour and film, and much more money. But two years is my limit. With those sorts of subjects, the scripts start leaving the ground eventually. There are limited amounts you can do. I mean, *Spooks*, one saw getting madder and mad-

der. So I was going anyway, my contract was up – and *Goldfinger* was a nice step to take.

I must have been the only person in England not to be wearing leather. Everybody was wearing leather then, but I didn't dare, for fear I'd be recognised. It was different then, there weren't so many television channels and there was still a certain distance between one-self and the public. Still, one had a terrible time if one went to Harrod's or something. It was very difficult – but nice difficult, I suppose.

When I got the call to be in the Bond film – I'm not very modest about it, I thought I was absolutely right for it. I am proud of having done it. At the time you just look at it as a job. It never occurred to me to ask for danger mon-ey or anything like that. Patrick MacNee always wor-ried terribly. 'Darling, why don't you fight like me, with a walking-stick?' And I thought, the whole point is that the ladies do all the tough stuff. He's lovely, though, Patrick.

The only problem they had with it was that I wasn't well-known in America. The tape didn't go out there.

There was an American late-night show – Johnny Car-son – I was over there to do an interview with him and their office kept badgering, badgering – would I throw Johnny? And you don't like to do it, in case they don't know how to fall, or whatever, and something dread-ful happens. Eventually, I said, I'll try him out before the show and see – if he could be thrown and live, you know. It was so funny. It so surprised the audience. And he did exactly what Sean does in the film – pulled my legs from under me, and played Sean's scene. That bit I wasn't expecting.

When I went to drama school and didn't have the money to do a full-time course, I used to go in my lunchtimes and in the evening – and I still finished the course at the same time as everybody else did, because I was so clever, haha! That's what acting's about – you have to do whatever's expected of you.

I'm about to do a one-person show about my life. Looking back, my brother was short and I was tall. He was a bit of a dreamer and he was always being set upon

by other boys. My father taught us to box when we were about four, five. I knocked out two boys, cold, because they attacked my brother – one in the playground, the other in our front garden. I knew what to do, and that was that. And I remember getting out of my car, in my twenties or thirties, and really going for someone, some boy who was attacking this smaller creature. I don't suppose I would now because they'd be carrying knives.

Judo is about balance and knowing which throw to do, in the circumstances. I know how to break people's hands and how not to get strangled. You should push their hands up and away from you, and then kick them in the shins as you do it, and then turn round and kick them in the balls and get out. But I don't know that playing these roles gave me any more confidence with men – I've always been pretty shy, really. Lots of actors are shy, that's why they're actors.

I did call a taxi driver out for a fight once. I was drunk at the time. Happily, he didn't get out, because I don't think I would have been much good at it. I did get called out by various chaps but they were always drink-taken. They'd say, 'C'mon outside, if you're so good'. It was men who weren't too confident about their potency. They couldn't bear to think that a girl could do it, really" ■

Previous page: *Goldfinger* director Guy Hamilton checks his angles before the famous fight scene between Blackman and Connery. This page: their stunt doubles get to grips, while left, Connery grapples with stuntwoman Phyllis Corner.

Stunt Arranger Bob Simmons
and his assistant watch as
Connery runs through the fight
scene. Phyllis Corner (right)
Honor Blackman's stunt double.

Pussy Galore (Honor Blackman) throws her head back having been "rolled in the hay" by Bond.

Honor Blackman and *Goldfinger* director Guy Hamilton relax on set during rehearsals for the now famous fight scene.

BOND STREET STYLE
by Dylan Jones

There has always been something economical about the way James Bond dresses. Sharp, yes. Controlled, obviously. But never, ever showy. Unlike his famous martinis, as a fashion plate Bond has never looked shaken or stirred. Never a flash of ostentatious, he has always been pared down, measured, almost Spartan. And while the well-dressed gentleman spy is certainly a thing of the past his signature style will be with us forever.

Bond is best described in Moonraker, where Fleming calls him: "The rather saturnine young man in his middle thirties… something a bit cold and dangerous in that face. Looks pretty fit [a] tough-looking customer." His classic outfit – his usual rig – meanwhile, was best sketched in The Man With the Golden Gun, the very last Bond novel: "Dark blue single breasted suit, white shirt, think black, knotted silk tie, black casuals". A man who drives an Amherst Villiers supercharged 4.5 litre Bentley.

And that is about it. Other than to say that Bond was well dressed without being particularly overdressed. Fleming was always fairly circumspect about his protagonist's wardrobe, which is perhaps why his books took so long to be turned into pictures.

The visual style of the early films was based on the Bond cartoon strip that first appeared in the Daily Express in 1958, during that long forgotten period when the paper still had some good ideas. Stylistically Dr. No, the first film, was certainly better than the first attempt to bring Bond to the screen. A year after Casino Royale was published in 1953, "Jimmy" Bond was played on American television by an actor called Barry Nelson. They changed his nationality (he was now a Yankee) his job (CIA agent) and – sin of all sins – his clothes, kitting him out in a loose-fitting, shawl-collared tuxedo and what looked suspiciously like a clip-on bow tie.

While he was a hero in print, it took the movies to turn Bond into a star, took Sean Connery's legendary swagger to turn the besuited British secret agent into a fully-fledged sex symbol and style icon. With *Dr. No*, Connery was suddenly the best-dressed man in the cinema. He wore Turnbull & Asser shirts with French cuffs, specially made by Michael Fish (who went on to open his own hugely influential shop, Mr Fish); he wore a Nehru jacket, and razor-sharp suits made for him by Anthony Sinclair in London's Conduit Street. Connery was both smart and casual, and the knitted short-sleeved shirt he wore when helping Ursula Andress out of the sea has been a casual-wear classic ever since.

He was influential in other ways because he always favoured two-piece tropical-weight suits (about 6-7oz) that offered serious mobility; men bought them in their hundreds of thousands; because he wore a white tuxedo it began filling the pages of countless fashion magazines. Such an icon was Connery that in 1996, American GQ devoted an issue to his interpretation of Bond style.

True to the books, Connery's style was always understated; in *Goldfinger*, the outfit he wears to drive his Aston Martin DB5 (gunmetal grey with leather oxblood

57

interior) consists of a tweed hacking jacket, plain cotton shirt, plain tie and heavy cavalry-twill trousers with cross pockets and narrow buttons, angled to fit neatly over his suede chukka boots. This reflected his military background and his need to be smartly turned out at all times. Pierce Brosnan, more than three decades later, echoed the off-duty military look in *GoldenEye*, in a navy-blue, cable-knit sweater, silk foulard cravat, narrow-leg moleskin trousers and Church's brown brogues. And Brosnan like every other custodian of Commander Bond's uniform, has expressed a liking for that most regimental of jackets, the blue blazer.

The early films were not just spy capers: they were also extended travelogues for a generation that had hardly been abroad, let alone tempted to do it in style. Everyone wanted in. So successful was Connery that he soon caused a flurry of imitation: James's Cobourne's Flint, Robert Vaughn's Napoleon Solo, Frank Sinatra's Tony Rome, Dean Martin's Matt Helm and Peter Wyngarde's Jason King. And so successful was the image that throughout the Sixties, dozens of manufacturers sought licences to label their products "007" or "James Bond" – shoes, shirts ties, suits, cologne, cigarette holders, even condoms. Bond advertised Jim Beam, Smirnoff and inspired the Dormeuil man, for years the most enduring male fashion icon. Boussac, France's most important

textile group, created a line of Bond raincoats, shirts and pyjamas bearing the 007 number, and also a line for boys with the moniker 003 ½.

When Connery tired of being an international clotheshorse he was replaced (briefly) by George Lazenby, whose main contribution to the sartorial legacy was the sky-blue two piece spandex ski suit, complete with white roll-neck top, that he wore in his only Bond outing *On Her Majesty's Secret Service*. Either that, or using his solid gold Rolex as a knuckle-duster.

Roger Moore chose some rather fine suits by Doug Hayward of Mount Street, Mayfair, although Moore's own predilection was for the sports jacket, which he wore with impunity throughout his tenure, from *Live And Let Die* in 1973 through to *A View To A Kill* in 1985. Particularly arresting were the Donegal jacket he chose for *The Man With The Golden Gun*. But it's his safari suits, blousons and slip-on shoes that we'll remember him for, a combination that is difficult to forgive, though strangely easy to admire. It is a testament to the

series' art directors and stylists that the Seventies films are so kitsch that Moore's wardrobe often seems tame by comparison.

Moore was replaced in the mid Eighties by the politically correct Shakespearian lounge lizard Timothy Dalton, a man who was never going to convincingly play a clotheshorse. He had a liking for slim knitted black ties and structureless suits, although he was too intent on playing with Bond's image to really be a hit with the public. Dalton became Bond during a time when the box-office heroes – Stallone, Willis and Schwarzenegger – were more interested in wearing T-shirts than suits no matter how unstructured, so even though *The Living Daylights* had a neat melancholy not seen since the Sixties, Dalton only lasted two films.

It is rather a shame that Dalton didn't feel happier in his character's skin, as he was potentially far more intriguing an actor than Brosnan, who on occasion was little but a more manly Moore in a better suit. In several ways Brosnan was the most traditional Bond yet,

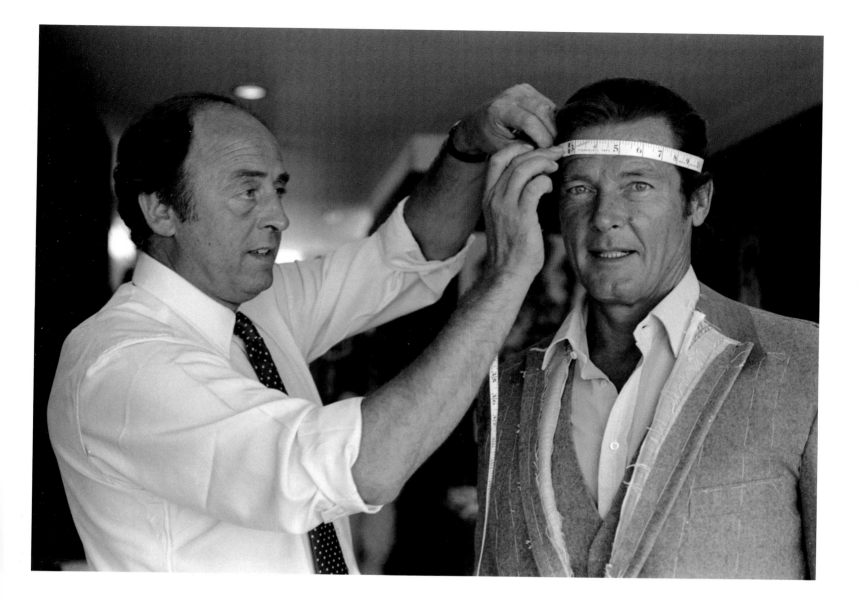

dressing in beautifully cut three-piece Brioni suits, Church's brogues and Jermyn Street shirts. He didn't look timely so much as rich: his style was unmistakably synonymous with expensiveness.

At the time, realistically this was the only way for Bond to go. In the Nineties the iconic spy/hoodlum/gangster film had become such a popular cliché, abused by everyone from Mike Myers to Quentin Tarantino, that one of the ways in which the Bond films could convincingly lift themselves above the morass of tongue-in-cheek, self referential movie iconography was by looking lush.

Instead, the producers went back to basics and hired a great-looking, rugged 38-year-old movie star called Daniel Craig. And the world spun again. With *Casino Royale*, Bond got his groove back again, particularly in the way he dressed. Craig immediately announced himself as a suit snob, one with a penchant for the work of Brunello Cucinelli: "They're so luxurious – they're light, great and seem to fit me. Buying off the peg, it can be a bit difficult to find something that fits you but I put on a Brunello Cucinelli and I didn't have to get it adjusted. It's the same with Tom Ford – if I put on his off the peg, they fit me like a glove. I can't be bothered waiting around for all the tailoring – unless you're getting a suit made."

And what did Craig consider to be the most stylish film of all? Well, oddly it wasn't a Bond movie. "Steve McQueen always had it," he says. "Look at *The Thomas Crown Affair* – it's one of the most stylish films there is. Certain movies of the late Sixties are stylish [because] suits were worn by everybody. It's not so much that way anymore. Suits are looked at more now as a business thing which is kind of a shame. If you're not wearing it just for work, you should try and trick it up a bit."

Craig cared about how he looked, what he wore, and how he was being shot while he was wearing it. He may have gone to great lengths to claim otherwise, but then he's Bond, and James Bond can say what he likes ∎

Dylan Jones is the editor of GQ

George Lazenby cut an
impressive figure modeling
menswear but failed to
make a mark as 007 –
unlike Pierce Brosnan.

Brosnan in beautifully cut
Brioni suits – a style that was
unmistakably expensive but
purists might argue English
tailoring from Saville Row
was more traditional Bond.
Overleaf: Daniel Craig,
photographed by O'Neill in
June 2012 for Esquire
magazine has kept Bond
apace with fashion.

THE GIRLS:
JILL MASTERSON
by Shirley Eaton

"I was 27 when I got the role of Jill Masterson in *Goldfinger*. Just back from holidaying in the South of France, all tanned and feeling good, my agent called and said that Harry Saltzman wanted to meet me.

He'd seen my work but wanted to know if I minded being nude and painted in gold! So long as it was done elegantly and I trusted it would be, I didn't mind.

It was lovely working with Sean. Very professional but at the same time relaxed, fun, sexy and the chemistry between us was wonderful. I was on the shoot for a week at Pinewood.

Due to the gold paint being terribly uncomfortable, Guy Hamilton the director shot that particular set up in one morning, very fast for those days. It was a closed set, but I remember there being so many paparazzi around, taking shots in between scenes. Extraordinary. As actors we just get on with the job not realizing at the time how important a film may turn out. Almost 50 years ago and that's the one film I'm known for still today, even though I made 21 films before *Goldfinger* and 7 after! On the day my friend, the actor Graham Stark happened to be on the next lot making a naval film with Richard Attenborough.

Apparently Sean said "oh come on the set, Shirley's about to do the gold naked scene." I was painted and ready to go when they walked into my dressing room. I was a little hyper and a bit cross with Graham but I laughed, went up and hugged him and his white naval uniform became covered in my gold silhouette! I had left my mark.

You couldn't have a Bond film without the Bond girls. Over the years they've changed, becoming less like a cookie on the side! They were very much like that in the beginning. Ursula Andress coming out of the sea was just one of those magical moments. She had such an innocence about her. She was my favourite Bond girl.

The first two Bond films did very well but nobody knew that *Goldfinger* was to become so successful and one of the best Sean made.

It was the beginning of big stuff and wonderful to be a part of. From the actors to the sets and gadgets, everything just came together which doesn't happen that often. It was a very special time in my life" ∎

Valerie Leon (*The Spy Who Loved Me,* 1977) in a scene with Peter Sellers
(*Revenge of The Pink Panther*) and Zena Marshall as Miss Taro (*Dr. No,* 1962).

Geraldine Chaplin the daughter of the famous Charlie, played an uncredited role in the Bond spoof *Casino Royale* (1967) before becoming a star in the 70s. Jacqueline Bisset was Miss Goodthighs in the same film.

Ursula Andress was the immortal Honey Ryder in *Dr. No* (1962) but showed her comedic talent in the *Casino Royale* parody of 1967 as the screen's first Vesper Lynd.

Jill St. John (this page and next) and George Lazenby relaxing by the poolside at her house in LA in 1969. Lazenby left the role and Sean was eventually coaxed back to play Agent 007 with a $1.2 million paycheck with which he started the charity The Scottish Educational Trust.

St John and Lazenby dated
during filming of Lazenby's
aborted second appearance as
007. Lazenby had been signed
for seven Bond movies but
disappeared into obscurity
while St John went on to star
in numerous television series.

THE ENGLISH GIRL
by Joanna Lumley

"I had been modelling from the age of 18, and by the time I was 21 I had a baby. I didn't want to be a model but I just drifted into it. In the 60's everyone was a model it seemed. I worked all the time, I loved it but I really wanted to be an actress. I couldn't see any way into it because I'd never been to drama school and with a baby couldn't do 42 weeks in rep to get an Equity card. I somehow wangled through it. Richard Johnson whom I met at a party said "I'm in a film at the moment which if you say one line in will get you your card.""

A stroke of luck! So I did that film with him, my one line being "Yes Mr. Robinson" followed by another small film and then my agent said they were casting for Bond girls and to go along and see Harry Saltzman.

It was a hot gorgeous day when I arrived at the doorstep of the South Audley street office just as Harry got out of his big Rolls Royce. The lift was broken so we had to go puff puff up the stairs, not speaking and stopping on every landing, and being a rather round fat man, by the time he sat at his desk he was purple from exertion. His only words were "You have the part" and I said "oh thank-you" and went all the way down the stairs again.

I was one of 12 Bond girls, the principle being Diana Rigg who marries Bond and then sadly gets killed. For all the love I have of the Bond movies *On Her Majesty's Secret Service* seems to be one of the best in terms of plot. We girls were the Angels of Death working for the dreaded Blowfelt played by Telly Savalas, all carrying vials of horrifying germs. Each girl representing their country. I was English girl, Jenny Hanley Irish girl, Anoushka Hempel was Aussie girl and we had one from Denmark, Israel, Japan, India, Africa and so forth. Now it had George Lazenby as Bond who had been a model and I think that after Sean had stopped playing the role they had thought let's just get a handsome hunk to do it. Bond can be played by anybody. Not so. He was okay, looking back on it he gave the performance as best he could do.

We were taken out to Switzerland for the duration of two months to the village of Murren, accessible only by funicular as there were no motor vehicles in the village. Across this vast valley was the village of Wengen, and the Jungfrau and the Eiger Mountains. Behind us was the Schilthorn which after filming, had a revolving restaurant on top. The deal was that the owners allowed the filming to take place there if by the end they would leave a restaurant that revolved. The whole area was roped off, all round Murren, nobody allowed except crew – that was massive. We had Olympic skiers to play Blofelt's henchmen with submachine guns as ski poles, and all us Bond lovelies!

Our hotel was a huge grand late 19th century British ski resort sort of place, not unlike a prison! We'd be up at 5am to be in make-up and then go 10,000 feet up the mountain to film, over the two months. We were paid £100 a week, which to me was a king's ransom. We were allowed one phone call home a week, we had Fridays

off and on Wednesday evenings they'd blackout the hotel ballroom and screen movies as there were no TV's or videos, nothing! Some of us had boyfriends who came out to visit. The now Marquis of Bath was pretty crazed with Sylvanna Enrikes who was a very tall beautiful black girl. He came out with his long wild hair and hippy beads!

We filmed from October to December and as it got colder and darker we weren't allowed to ski in case we broke anything. Dear old Lazenby who was a fit bloke couldn't do anything either. He was rather a lost soul and I felt that he might be a bit lonely as he and Diana didn't really hit it off. So I became a sort of a mate. He was always trying to play Hey Jude on the guitar and he'd say "hey Lumley, hey Jude"!

He invited me along to the very first dinner he and Diana had together as he was afraid he wouldn't be able to keep the conversation up. She was quite grand, a trained actress with the RSC and he just a big Australian. The funny thing is she'd been an *Avengers* Girl and after Linda Thorson I took on the role!

When the filming was over and we all said our good-byes, what struck me was it was so far away from the film's release that you'd almost lost touch with it. As I was quite good at copying voices when it came to the post-synching of the film they got me in to do some of the girls' voices for the scenes we were all in together as all the girls had gone back to different places. So I felt more linked to the film than maybe some of them had.

There's something you can never take away from being part of Bond.

Despite going on to do grander things none of them stick the way that film did. It's remained as bright as day to me. The sense of having been a part of it is the magic that will be remain with me forever" ■

Jill St. John, left, as Tiffany
Case in *Diamonds Are Forever*,
photographed in her hotel room
during location shooting in
Amsterdam. Diana Rigg,
above, became the only
actress to play Mrs. James
Bond in 1969's *On Her
Majesty's Secret Service*.

MISS CARUSO
by Madeline Smith

"The summer before I was cast in *Live And Let Die* I had been in an episode of *The Persuaders*. I lose track of time as back then I trotted from job to job. I was fairly dire but incredibly lucky! A couple of quick scenes with Tony Curtis and Roger Moore. I had a lovely time. I think of The Persuaders in full sunshine! I didn't know that I had made any impression but Roger subsequently recommended me for my role in *Live And Let Die*. I do not even remember having to audition, just being asked would I like to do it. "Yes, thank-you very much indeed!"

It was a three day shoot, a mixture of the wardrobe and the bed. I played an Italian spy, I'm not even sure I had a name. I was just 'beautiful girl' in the script. Miss Caruso was plonked on to the titles afterwards. We kick off in bed, very modest and decorous when all of a sudden M and Moneypenny arrive to lay the plot. I scuttle sheepishly in my frilly knickers into the wardrobe picking up my clothes as I go. When they eventually leave, Bond opens the wardrobe and there I am in this ghastly blue dress! I am on record now for saying that the dress was hideous. There were additional bosoms, white plastic inserts on top of my own, to make them stand proud! Almost regal looking.

Bond unzips the dress with his magic watch and I deliver my one line "Finalemente" ie, finally! That took several takes as the business with the watch didn't work

immediately. There was a nylon thread going down the back of the dress but because the material was so thick the zip would not undo. Derek Meddings, the special effects chap was lying between my legs pulling down on the thread whilst Bond smiles at the top! So a lot of laughter and several goes and of course a now famous watch as a result.

Between takes Roger would go off to rehearse a fight scene in one corner of the studio. I remember he brought on to the set the music for the film.

He played it on a tiny cassette player and exclaimed "isn't this the best score! "It was the very first time any of us heard it. The fantastic theme tune by Wings.

Roger was my favourite Bond. He was a gentleman, very masculine and didn't take himself seriously. After all half the joy of the Bond films is that we are not supposed to take them seriously. He did though have a certain edge, a menace as Bond.

My favourite Bond girl has to be Britt Ekland. Adorable looking and delightful as 'Mary Goodnight'. The Bond Girls have become more sophisticated than we all were. They are required to act and be involved a lot more these days. Getting down and dirty in every sense. They are certainly put through their paces, whilst we were perky little sweethearts decorating the place rather than acting our socks off!" ■

"We were perky little sweethearts decorating the place" says Madeline Smith who appeared as Miss Caruso in one of the most comical and engaging Bond seduction scenes of all time – a scene Moore rehearsed with relish (previous page).
Overleaf: Jane Seymour (Solitaire) bewitched Moore in the same movie, *Live And Let Die*.

MARY GOODNIGHT
by Britt Ekland

"As a child I was brought up on Ian Fleming's books. My father would sit in his library in Sweden and read them in English. Later, when I saw Ursula Andress in *Dr. No* I thought I want to do that. Not for the sexiness of it or the bikini but because it was such a stunning and powerfully visual image on film.

By the time I'd read The Man With The Golden Gun I had been in loads of films. One day in January in the 70's I called Cubby's office requesting to see him. We'd never met but I was known. I just happened to live in Mayfair at the time, close to his office on Mount Street. So I dressed up like a secretary in little kitten heels, a long grey skirt with a white blouse and cardigan, hair in a bun, no make up and walked there. He said "We don't use the book per se but take the title and develop a script, but thank-you for coming." As he escorted me out Roger Moore appeared from another room, we said hello and that was that.

Several months later, on a return flight from the States where I had been making a movie I read in the English papers 'Swedish actress in new Bond film'. At first I thought it's probably me, but then when I read Maud Adams' name I was absolutely devastated! I later read that she was to be the villain's girlfriend.

When I got the call from my agent saying Cubby wanted to see me I thought it would be to apologize that I did not get the film, but when we met again he just came towards me with a script and said "You are Mary Goodnight" and that was that.

Maud and I first met on the plane and we became instant friends and still are to this day. She is from the far north of Sweden and is my complete opposite. I like beautiful things, I like to party and drink but she is and was very serious. Still, we became soul mates.

Shooting on location from April to June in Thailand and then Hong Kong was very interesting. We shot on the islands that then were nameless. They looked like giant teeth. I believe they are now called The James Bond Islands. There was nothing in Phuket at that time, no hotels, just endless beaches.

Maud and I had to stay in a vacant brothel! The "girls" had been sent away. There were these neon lights outside the windows that attracted these huge flying critters that terrified us, flapping around outside. We have flies the size of a thumb nail, these were four times as big.

We were always scared of Guy Hamilton the director, he was a hard task master. We'd joke around with Roger who made us feel we were his equal but with Guy it was different.

Christopher Lee was also very serious and there was to be no mention of Hammer films! I'd worked with Christopher on a film called *The Wicker Man* and at the time was 4 months pregnant and had very nice big breasts.

Cubby had seen me in the film, but was disappointed when I was cast in Bond as I was dead thin and so he remedied that by making sure I would eat a lot at the Saturday night spaghetti feasts he'd give for cast and crew.

It was an amazing shoot but it didn't change my life career-wise and financially it was somewhat ruinous as I had my children with me for a time and had to pay for their travel, accommodation and the nannies salary. Still for a Swede the idea of going to the Far East was very appealing and I had a fantastic time" ∎

Britt Ekland (previous pages) thought her friend Maud Adams (right) had beaten her to the role of Mary Goodnight before Cubby Broccoli called to tell her she'd won the part, while Adams would play Christopher Lee's girlfriend Andrea Anders in *The Man With The Golden Gun*. The girls stayed in a vacant brothel in Thailand during filming.

Alexandra Bastedo was one of an enormous star-studded cast of the 1967 spoof *Casino Royale* before making her name in the television series *The Champions*.

Beginning her film career in 1963, Alexandra Bastedo appeared twice with Roger Moore in *The Saint* TV series before becoming a Bond girl in the 1967 spoof *Casino Royale*.

Barbara Bach (above) starred
with two other Bond girls,
Claudine Auger and
Barbara Bouchet in the
mystery La Tarantola Dal
Ventre Nero before her role
in *The Spy Who Loved Me*.

American model and actress Barbara Bach played Russian spy Anya Amasova in *The Spy Who Loved Me*. The producers initially approached a young Steven Speilberg to direct. The Pinewood studios soundstage was so enormous that Stanley Kubrick secretly visited to advise on lighting the sets. Bach went on to marry Ringo Starr.

Overleaf: British model Caroline Munro turned her back on Hollywood after her much lauded role as Naomi, the seductive killer who tried to gun down Bond from her helicopter in *The Spy Who Loved Me*. Munro preferred to stay in England to be close to her family. She was notably, the first woman to be killed by Bond in character. She had enjoyed a little known role in the 1967 *Casino Royale* spoof.

Jenny Flex was May Day's henchwoman in *A View To A Kill* in 1985. She was played by Irish actress Alison Doody who was 18 and the youngest woman ever to play a Bond girl.

KARA MILOVY
by Maryam d'Abo

"At the age of 26 I was making a film in Germany with Maximillian Schell and Mick Jagger called *Laughter In The Dark*. About a month into the shooting the film collapsed because the money never appeared. I had lost a lot of weight for the part and my hair was cut into a 1920's bob for the role.

I came back to London looking very different to the screen test I'd taken part in six months before leaving for Munich. I'd done a day's work at Pinewood feeding the lines in a screen test for the actor testing for Bond. The film was *From Russia With Love*, Cubby Broccoli was there and John Glenn was directing the scene. I had long hair at the time and looked much younger than 26.

I happened to be at my health club drying my hair one day and Barbara Broccoli, whom I knew through mutual friends, said hello. The next thing I know my agent calls me and says that the Bond people would like to see me for the leading role in *The Living Daylights*.

It transpired that MGM had called Cubby to say they had seen twenty minutes of footage of a German film that needed funding and that the girl in it corresponded to the role of Kara Milovy, and that they should see me. So off I went to meet them. I nearly fell off my seat when I got the role. I'm 5ft 6in, Bond girls were glamorous, athletic, 5ft 10in, like Grace Jones and I never saw myself like that.

Kara Milovy is Czechoslovakian and a cellist, dying to get to the West. She is involved with the villain who has promised her he'll get her papers to do so and pursue her career, but first she must kill someone for him. Bond tries to find out about the villains through her.

I had more of a story line with Bond as I think in the 80's they were trying to create more of a relationship with the new Bond played by Timothy Dalton. I did not have any super powers, I was just a musician caught up in Bond's world.

It was a lovely five month shoot starting out with two weeks in Vienna where I had to rehearse and work with the symphony orchestra learning intense pieces of music on the cello, then Tangiers, the Moroccan desert and finishing off at Pinewood. I learned to horseback ride properly too, the things you do to be a Bond girl!

There were difficult moments, like bringing arms into Morocco for the shoot which proved tricky, but Barbara dealt with that. I believe it was her first film as associate producer, and fun moments such as Cubby flying in all this pasta from Italy and taking over the kitchens where we were staying to organize big pasta nights for everyone. The crew being so fed up with Moroccan food and stomach issues.

Cubby would give the most fantastic parties in the desert, it was like old Hollywood and all of us have very fond memories.

Timothy was extremely supportive and professional. He knew how nervous I was to be on a big production like that, it's a big machine you know, but one that I was extremely lucky to be a part of.

It also opened doors for me especially in America for if I hadn't done Bond I would never have gone to LA for the film's publicity and hence would not have landed the role in a pilot that became a series. So my life changed drastically as I left Europe to work in America for the next ten years" ∎

Minnie Driver landed the role
of Russian nighclub singer
Irina in *GoldenEye* (1995).

Famke Jannsen was the
edgiest Bond girl to date,
playing *GoldenEye's*
sadosexual assassin Xenia
Onatopp, while Izabella
Scorupco provided Pierce
Brosnan's love interest
as Natalya Simonova.

"Pierce Brosnan is one of
the most professional and
charming men I've worked
with," recalls Terry O'Neill,
"and I don't think there has
ever been a sexier pairing –
or more provocative Bond girls
than Famke and Izabella.
They have to be two of the
most beautiful women ever
to grace a Bond movie."

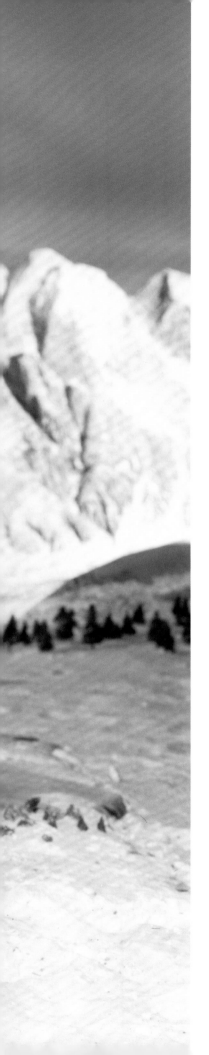

"Izabella was a Vogue model – and you can see it in this picture. So many actresses are nervous about being shot but Izabella was sexually calm and natural. She just knew she was beautiful – and would look beautiful. It wasn't arrogance, just confidence" recalls O'Neill.

ROGER MOORE
by George Perry

An enduring myth has it that Roger Moore auditioned for *Dr. No,* losing out to Sean Connery who was three years younger. It did not happen. At the time Moore was fully committed to playing *The Saint* on television. Yet, fourteen years later, in 1975 after six official (and one unofficial) turns as 007, when Connery decided to step down, unusually, the older man took over and Roger Moore was signed for *Live And Let Die.* He was amused to learn from Cubby Broccoli that his name had indeed been down on the short list of actors for consideration back in 1961.

Connery may have defined the role in a particular way, but Moore was noticeably different, a tall, smooth, handsome Englishman with a deep, melodious voice. He was elegant, charming, well-mannered and witty. Although he had briefly studied at RADA (Lois Maxwell, the original Moneypenny, was a contemporary), he was renowned for a self-deprecating, laidback, un-histrionic acting style. Had he been set the clubland test of stopping a Pall Mall taxi with minimum effort he would have won with ease, an arched eyebrow and slight tilt of the head being quite sufficient. He was often mocked, particularly by the satirical TV show *Spitting Image,* for acting only with his eyebrows, and was not offended in the slightest.

For someone who looked as if born to wear a dinner jacket his antecedents were surprisingly ordinary. He was born in Stockwell in 1927, the son of a London policeman and part-educated until the war at Battersea Grammar School. Like Connery he had various jobs, even lorry-driving (years later as 007 he surprised the stunt crew by his expert handling of a big truck in *Live And Let Die*). He drifted into films, graduating from extra to walk-ons, then was called up for national service in the army, where he gained a commission in the Royal Army Service Corps. Afterwards he persisted with acting, and eked out a living posing in advertisements for knitwear and toothpaste. His early movies were mostly instantly forgettable, and his break came via television, in *Ivanhoe* and *The Alaskans,* and as James Garner's English cousin in *Maverick.* The shrewd TV mogul Lew Grade recognised his potential and made a star out of him as Simon Templar, *The Saint,* in a six-season series which, although British-made, was shown extensively in the United States. Only occasionally did he venture into films, the most notable of which was the intriguing fantasy-thriller *The Man Who Haunted Himself* (1970), perhaps his best serious role. He returned to television to team up with Tony Curtis in *The Persuaders,* a hit in Europe but not in America. It did however make him the world's highest-paid TV actor.

There had been a hiccup in the Bond saga when the Australian George Lazenby had taken over the role from Sean Connery for *On Her Majesty's Secret Service* (1969). His performance ("like a brick-built dunny") was not popular with the public, and to be fair had the difficulty of following in the wake of someone who had perfected the role. In any case Connery, with legal

differences settled, came back to play Bond in *Diamonds Are Forever* (1971) but thereafter called it a day, until he returned as Bond in the nonconformist production *Never Say Never Again* (1983).

Roger Moore, after a few rounds on the exercise treadmill, then made his 007 debut with *Live and Let Die* (1973). Very wisely no attempt was made to mould him on Connery, instead more sardonic quips and caustic asides were written in. Although purists were sniffy at what they saw as the dilution of a familiar brand, the popular view was that his cool charm and laidback drollery gave 007 a new and agreeable dimension. The Moore style worked even better in *The Man With The Golden Gun* (1974) where Bond had a worthy enemy in Scaramanga (Christopher Lee). The next was *The Spy Who Loved Me* (1977), which had a troubled gestation with the departure of the co-producer Harry Saltzman and Guy Hamilton, who had directed four Bonds in a row, also drawn-out litigation with Kevin McClory. For a while Steven Spielberg was talked

of as director ("we'll have to see how the fish picture turns out") before Lewis Gilbert, a Bond veteran (*You Only Live Twice*) was assigned. Its ultimate scriptwriter Christopher Wood removed all traces of the Connery Bond to allow Moore to play the hero totally his own way. At a mere 6ft 1in, Moore was also obliged to confront a 7ft 2in steel-toothed adversary called Jaws (Richard Kiel) who proved popular enough to earn a reprise in the next.

An enormous stage was built at Pinewood, the world's largest, to accommodate pens for nuclear submarines. The 007 Stage would in subsequent years be twice burned down, and twice rebuilt, and stands today as the Albert R. Broccoli Stage. Surprisingly the next, *Moonraker* (1979) was not filmed at Pinewood at all but in Paris for taxation reasons, and is the only Bond film to have sequences, including the mandatory spectacular finale, set in outer space, the producers having been conditioned by the stupendous success of *Star Wars* (1977). Moore gave his by now customary

display of insouciance in the face of unimaginable perils, but it was felt that now the real stars were the gadgetry, the special effects, and the spectacular set creations of Ken Adam. Moore would go on to make three more Bond films, *For Your Eyes Only* (1981), *Octopussy* (1983), which almost coincided with Connery's *Never Say Never Again* and managed to surpass its box-office take, and *A View To A Kill* (1985).

The 007 Stage, first burned to the ground during production of the Ridley Scott film *Legend*, was rebuilt and re-opened for *A View To A Kill* with an enormous set of a mine belonging to the villain Zorin (Christopher Walken). Invited press watched the shooting. I remember Bond racing athletically and making a flying leap attempting to rescue Grace Jones from a retreating mine cart laden with a primed bomb. Take after take, he did it without flagging. Not bad for his age one would have thought. Except Moore, in the same outfit, had quietly joined us, also to watch his energetic stunt double. "Does it rather well, doesn't he?" he comment-

ed in his amiable way. But then he always tried to avoid doing any running himself, on the grounds that his gait was too clumsy.

In fact he was by now 58, the oldest Bond ever, and remarked that his love interest had a mother younger than him. Gracefully he stepped down, handing on the torch to Timothy Dalton. He had played Bond in seven films, as many as Connery, including the one outside the official list. Although Moore's career continued his glory days were over. When he was knighted in 2003 it was not for acting but for his humanitarian work. Audrey Hepburn near death had asked him to take over her role as UNICEF goodwill ambassador for the world's children, and he has since embraced various charitable causes with zealous enthusiasm.

His private life has been colourful. As a baby-faced junior officer in 1946 he had married a Streatham ice skater six years his senior who had changed her name to Doorn Van Steyn in order to sound Dutch. On the way up the career ladder he met the popular Welsh

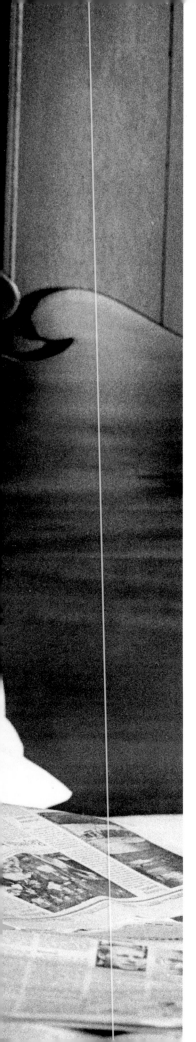

Previous page: Moore in the shark tank fight scene with Yaphet Koto in his debut Bond movie, *Live And Let Die*. This page: breakfast before Bond – the star and photographer O'Neill became firm friends.

song-belter Dorothy Squires, twelve years older than him, who installed him in a mansion and ensured he met the right people. It was a tempestuous union that became legendarily acrimonious with the years. He eventually left her for an Italian actress called Luisa Mattioli who would give him three children. Squires fell from the top of the tree when the younger Shirley Bassey seized the Welsh diva title, and became litigious and alcoholic. Towards the end of her life Moore paid for the medical bills for her cancer treatment. In time Mattioli's magic also wore off and he divorced her in 1993 to marry a wealthy Scandinavian, Kiki Tholstrup, and as an octogenarian spends his time with her in homes in Monaco, Switzerland and Denmark. Although an exile and like Connery immune from the British tax regime he firmly supports the Cameron Tories. He claims his right-of-centre views stem from the sense of social order handed down to him from his father who, it should be remembered, was a police officer ■

On location in New
Orleans during filming
of *Live And Let Die*.

Roger Moore and his ex-wife
Luisa in the south of France.

141

Hot dogs
Plain ·35
Dressed ·50
Corn dog ·40
Hamburger ·65
Cheeseburger ·70
Roll ·40
·35
·50

Moore's debut movie as Bond starred some of the most colourful villains ever to confront 007. Yaphet Kotto (bottom right) played two roles as Mr. Big and Dr. Kananga, Julius Harris was Tee Hee, his handless henchman (top left) and Geoffrey Holder as Baron Samedi and Earl Jolly Brown as Whisper (top right).

Gloria Hendry (left) as CIA
agent Rosie Carver, and
Jane Seymour (right) were
007's love interests in the movie.
While Seymour took the honours
for acting, Hendry stole the
show for becoming Bond's first
African-American lover.

Moore wrestles with a
'venomous' snake above.
Geoffrey Holder, left, the
Trinidadian actor who played
voodoo-practicing Baron
Samedi was cast not only
for his height (6"6') and
booming basso voice but
his abilities as a dancer.

THE CARS
by Joe Dunn

The name's Yeaggy. Harry Yeaggy. Three years ago an Ohio businessman proved that money is no object when it comes to owning a piece of James Bond exotica. He got carried away at a London auction and bid a superspy expense account worthy £2.6m for the Aston Martin DB5 that 007 drove in the 1964 film *Goldfinger*.

It's a lot of money, but others have paid far more to have their name associated with celluloid's most famous car. Ever since Sean Connery first revved up the DB5 complete with ejector seat, revolving number plates and machine guns, the world hasn't been able to get enough of the Bond cars. From BMWs to Lotus's, they have become the ultimate movie marketing machines with car companies competing, and paying enormous sums, to ensure that 007's Savile Row clad behind sits in their burnished leather seat.

It wasn't always like that. In fact, it was once the opposite. Before filming *Goldfinger*, the production company had originally pencilled in Connery driving a Bentley. This remained true to Ian Fleming's novels where Bond's first car was a 1933 4.5 litre Bentley, with a supercharger by Amherst Villiers. The Crewe car maker reportedly agreed to loan the car for the film – but would charge the usual hire rates. Hardly what the producers had in mind, so instead they turned to Aston Martin, a rival maker in classic English sports cars, and the unnamed manager at Bentley took his place alongside Dick Rowe the man who turned down The Beatles.

In any case, the choice of Aston Martin proved inspired (even if there were mutterings among the faithful that having an Aston in a talkie was a little declasse). The gun-metal grey DB5 with an enlarged 4.0 litre engine, was already a supreme grand tourer even before Bond. It was aimed at the men about town who might fancy a jaunt across the continent perhaps with their mistress in tow. And it was fast – by the day's standards at least: a top speed of 145mph and an acceleration from standstill to 60mph in 7.1sec put it in the top flight of cars. For comparison a 1964 Ford Anglia – the sort of car a middle class housewife might drive – had a theo-

retical top speed of 74mph and reaching 60mph took a glacial 23sec.

The DB5 has become the signature Bond car: it appeared in *Goldfinger, Thunderball, GoldenEye, Tomorrow Never Dies* and *Casino Royale*. It was also used by Roger Moore, on eyebrow arching form as the James Bond parody character in *The Cannonball Run* and, more recently, there have been a slew of video games featuring the car. And although marketing was in its infancy when the film was released, the potential of combining brand with Bond wasn't entirely lost: Corgi Toys cast a miniature version of the DB5 after the release of the film which became the best selling toy of 1964.

Despite its success, Connery wasn't confined to the Aston. It's best to skate over distinctly un-superspy suave Sunbeam Alpine he drove in the first Bond film, *Dr. No* (it didn't even have any alterations from Q) but the green DBS that he rigged in *Diamonds Are Forever* (1971) had some merit, not least a stinking great V6 engine with a meaty Aston growl. If you can't remember

it, you are not alone. It is Aston's forgotten car: changing tastes meant the DBS was already retro looking 40 years ago, a trick only the brown overall wearing Aston engineers of the 70's could pull off. It was also an ill-fated car: George Lazenby had a souped-up version for *On Her Majesty's Secret Service* (1969), but Q had omitted to include bulletproof glass, resulting in Bond's new bride getting shot in the final scene. Lazenby and the Aston were also history.

More memorably was the Mustang Mach 1 rental car Connery flips on to two wheels in Las Vegas in *Diamonds Are Forever* (1971). The scene features one of the classic continuity errors too: the Mustang tips onto its right hand side wheels on the way going into the alley, but emerges tipped onto the left hand side wheels.

In the late 70's with Roger Moore, Bond's cars moved up a gear. Gone was any notion that a British spy came with a classic sense of taste; in came more modish choices. And in 1977, with the release of *The Spy Who Loved Me*, you didn't get much more mod-

151

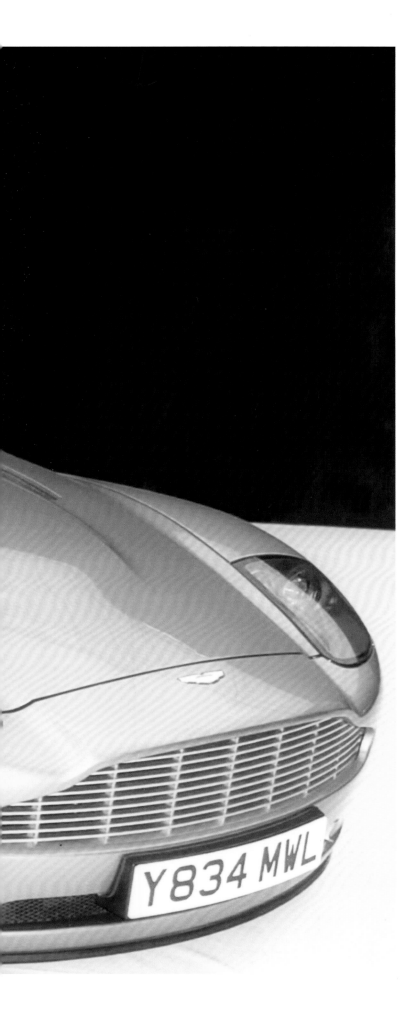

ish than a Lotus Esprit with the capacity to turn into a mini submarine. According to Lotus legend Donovan McLauchlan, the company's PR man, had been tipped off that the Bond movie was scheduled for Pinewood studios. He took a pre-production Esprit to the studios, tipped security and left the prototype in the most visible place he could find. Sure enough, it wasn't long before the production staff saw the car and asked if the company could provide one for Bond.

It was an audacious move from the British company, then still run by Colin Chapman – the maverick car designer – but it paid off: after the film's release Lotus was swamped with calls from potential customers, many of whom had never heard of the Norfolk firm before. Overnight the Esprit became a sell out with a three year waiting list.

The love affair between Lotus and Bond was short-lived, however. Starting with *Moonraker* in 1979 – a sad attempt to capitalise on the success of *Star Wars* – the Moore Bond films began suffering chronic genre fatigue. The most obvious symptom of this was the producers attempts to parody their own films, and by 1981 and *For Your Eyes Only*, Bond was reduced to performing a car chase for laughs in a Citroen 2CV.

Fleming would probably not have approved. As a young man in London, he took his cars very seriously. He owned a succession of dashing motors, ranging from a Standard tourer with an enamelled Union Jack on its nose, through a second-hand black Buick sports saloon, to a supercharged Graham Paige convertible coupe. After the war, he owned several British saloons: a Morris Oxford, a Hillman Minx and an Armstrong-

Siddeley Sapphire. He even dabbled with American muscle cars, driving a two door Ford Thunderbird – a car that Ann Fleming memorably described as "above our price bracket and below our age range".

Moore, was also beginning to look a little old for the Bond franchise and with his departure the movies and cars returned to safer, and more serious ground. Timothy Dalton was given a sombre Aston Martin Vantage Volante which boasted retractable snow spikes and wheel-mounted lasers but despite Q's best efforts the films – like the car company which had recently been bought by Ford, seemed to have lost their mojo.

Enter Pierce Brosnan to liven up the franchise in er, a German hairdressers car. The BMW Z3 seen in *GoldenEye* (blink and you'll miss it) was the first non-British car to be used as Bond's primary mode of transport. The reason you see so little of it was the car wasn't actually ready: it went on sale in 2006 and since the prototype seen in the film was virtually priceless, very little actual driving was allowed. Bond fans were not im-

pressed and neither were car fans: when the car eventually went on sale it was dismissed as an underpowered and overstyled plaything for people who didn't like cars. Quite what 007 was doing in it was a mystery although it is worth noting that its appearance brought the German company 10,000 advance orders worth some £190m.

BMW dismiss claims that they paid the film makers to feature their cars. Instead the agreement was rather more nuanced: the car company was obliged to fund a six-month Bond-related advertising campaign to tie in with the film's release effectively becoming a marketing partner. The deal covered three films which meant that in *Tomorrow Never Dies* (1997), Bond drives a BMW 750i, a rather boring executive saloon, while in *The World Is Not Enough* (1999) he gets a Z8 roadster; better than the Z3, but only just. For many the fate of the Z8 – chopped in half by helicopter blades – was a fitting end to Bond's dalliance with BMW.

Sanity or at least tradition was restored in *Die An-*

other Day in 2002 with Bond once again behind the wheel of an Aston, this time a V12 Vanquish. At the time it was reported that Ford paid the film makers $35m to get the brand back on the screen as part of a three film deal. If so they got their money's worth. Leaving aside the Aston, car fans couldn't help noticing that only five cars in the entire film did not belong to either Ford or Ford's Premier Automotive Group (which at the time owned Aston Martin, Jaguar, Land Rover, Volvo). Of those five – including a Ferrari F355, a Lamborghini Diablo and Porsche 911 none makes it through the film without suffering serious damage. Although Ford was not the only one (around 24 companies paid to have their brands used by Bond) perhaps it was no surprise, that *Die Another Day*, earned the sobriquet *Buy Another Day*.

By the time of *Casino Royale* (2006), the first Bond film starring Daniel Craig, little secret was being made of the fact that Bond's new car (a DBS) was as much about marketing as motors. In a carefully choreographed se-

quence the DBS model was unveiled to public amid much Bond fanfare just prior to the film's release. Ulrich Bez, the company's chairman said: "The DBS continues our proud association with James Bond. It is explosive power in a black tie and has its own unique character which will equal that of James Bond."

The DBS was kept for *Quantum Of Solace* in 2008 and no one is betting against Aston supplying a new car for the upcoming *Skyfall* film, which is slated for release in late 2012. Certainly at least one Aston is pegged to make an appearance: the DB5 bought by Harry Yeaggy is said to be making a cameo appearance in the film as if to prove that the car is as much a part of Bond as the improbably named women, the tux and the Walther PPK.

Such sentimentality would confuse the superspy's creator. According to Fleming, Bond's attitude to cars was as cold as his attitude to women. He "refused to be owned by any car. A car, however splendid, was a means of locomotion… and it must at all times be ready to locomote" ■

THE SPOOF
by George Perry

Think bad films, and the first *Casino Royale* from 1967 is likely to spring to mind. Is it as awful as received opinion has it? It has been called the most indulgent movie ever made, and it was certainly one of the costliest – $12 million in its day, a monumental over-run since its already over-generous budget was only half that.

Through legal complications the film rights to Ian Fleming's first novel had ended up with Charles K. Feldman. He had hoped to make a deal with Eon Productions to co-produce. When that failed he tried to lure Sean Connery, but the salary demanded was considered impossible. So rather than compete with what by then was a well-established franchise, Feldman decided to make his film as a spoof, a James Bond send-up. Many writers were asked their thoughts, even giants such as Ben Hecht, Billy Wilder and Terry Southern, and not just one director, but a five-strong posse was recruited, among them John Huston, Ken Hughes and Joseph McGrath, with poor Val Guest charged with the unattainable task of making their melange cohere.

The storyline was totally chaotic, with seven actors, some female, playing James Bond as a ruse to confuse SMERSH. The echt Bond was portrayed by David Niven, as a retired hero of Mafeking with a love child by Mata Hari, and recalled to duty by M (John Huston) in what should have been his dotage. The method of persuasion is explosive destruction of his stately pile which also carries off M himself. Bond is then assailed by M's feisty Scottish widow (Deborah Kerr) who storms his bedroom in a sexy black negligee crying "Comfort me, Jimmy". She is actually a SMERSH agent. Vesper (Ursula Andress) engages a baccarat expert (Peter Sellers) to become another 007 and bring financial ruin to Le Chiffre (Orson Welles) at the Casino Royale tables – the only sequence that has any relevance at all to Fleming's book. This Bond is seized by SMERSH and subjected to hallucinogenic torture by a battalion of Scottish pipers. They even somehow manage to incorporate a flying saucer sequence.

The cast dazzles – among the stunning women are Joanna Pettet, Daliah Lavi, Jacqueline Bisset and Barbara Bouchet. Stars such as William Holden, Charles Boyer, George Raft, even Peter O'Toole, drift in as though they were passing by and at a loose end. The casino itself is located atop a vast underground complex from which Bond's shy and awkward nephew Jimmy Bond (Woody Allen), alias Dr. Noah, is intent on world domination, but inadvertently swallows an atomic hiccup pill. A pitched battle joined by hordes of mounted cowboys and Indians, and the French Foreign Legion (a cameo by Jean-Paul Belmondo) reaches its climax when everything explodes and the entire cast ascends to the celestial fields, except for Jimmy who contentedly floats down to a warmer place.

So many writers and so many directors were involved, and appeared to be working in isolation from each other, the incoherence is unsurprising. When I first saw it at a Sixties press screening I thought it

A contact sheet from one of the hundreds of rolls of film Terry O'Neill shot at three London studios used to shoot *Casino Royale* in 1967. Ursula Andress showed a talent for comedy – and a refreshing lack of modesty.

was an unspeakable mess, a view shared by all around me. The filming, which extravagantly used the stages of Pinewood, Shepperton and MGM Borehamwood, had turned into a nightmare, largely because the egomaniacal and out-of-control Sellers kept disappearing for days at a time, and had developed a pathological antipathy to Orson Welles. Peter Sellers and Orson Welles appear together in only one set up. Immediately after it was shot Sellers disappeared without trace for three weeks. He was actually chasing Britt Ekland. And after looking at Terry's pictures on pages 104-105 who could blame him!

And yet, amidst the inchoate confusion there were occasional jokes that worked, and momentary flashes of visual brilliance. I was particularly taken by the monochromatic lobby of an East Berlin spy school extravagantly decked out with slanted, jagged trapezoids like a set from *The Cabinet Of Dr. Caligari*. In any case, the views of the critics hardly mattered. *Casino Royale* made a very respectable profit, and Burt Bacharach's theme tune, as well as the song "The Look of Love" sung by Dusty Springfield, zoomed up the music charts. Revisiting it again after years of conditioning by Monty Python, Terry Gilliam and Austin Powers I still marvel that so much talent could have been expended on such a turkey. But then there's no justice, least of all in the film business ■

A stunning shot of the moment Sir James Bond (retired) is "persuaded" to return to work by British intelligence which has decided the only way to wrest him from the comfort of his stately pile is by blowing it up.

On set for *Casino Royale*: His little thermometer – Buttercup (Angela Scoular) tests the bathwater for Sir James Bond (David Niven) just like she did for her father, McTarry – M (played by John Huston). Two years later Angela would make her second Bond girl appearance as Ruby Bartlett opposite George Lazenby in *On Her Majesty's Secret Service*.

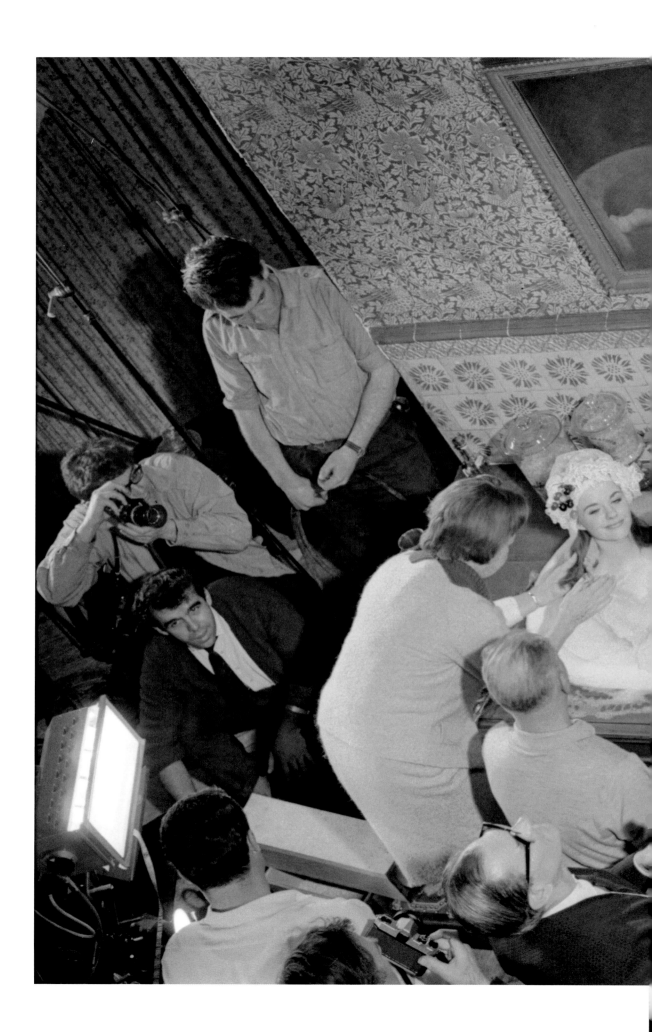

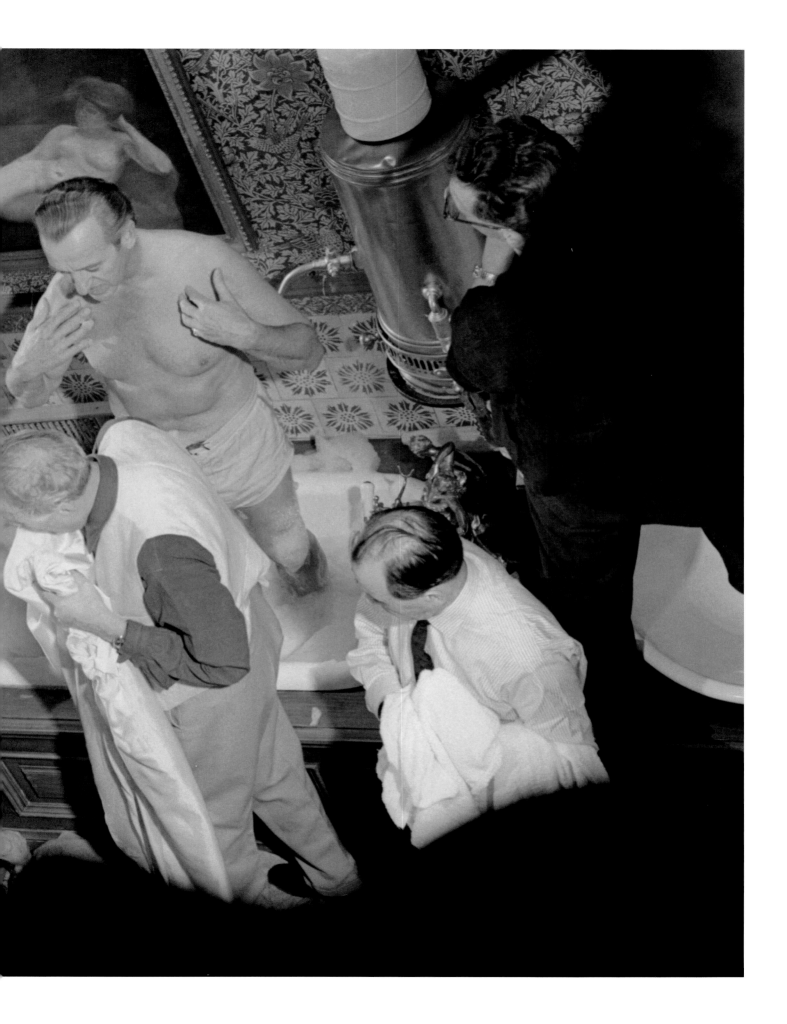

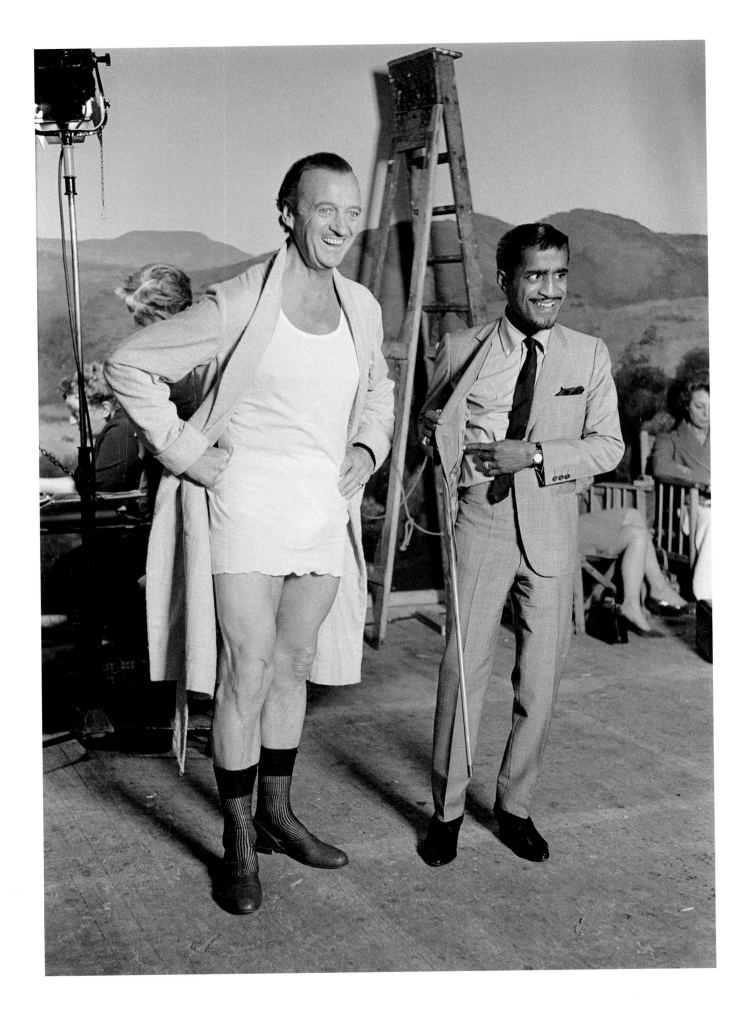

Casino Royale was as much
fun off set as on. From
Sammy Davis Junior turning
up to visit his pal David Niven
to Sellers goofing around.

Perhaps the only time a Lotus Formula 3 car has ever sported James Bond's name as a driver, and the only time the casino in Monte Carlo has been rebuilt in a studio.

171

If you're going to climb into
a Lotus racing car you
might as well hire the great
Stirling Moss in a walk-on
role to show you how to do it
and if you were ever unsure
that the first *Casino Royale*
was a spoof, then the fact that
Moss played Sellers' chauffeur
should dispel any doubt.

Casino Royale gave Sellers and Andress (above) the opportunity to parade their full comedic talents, although perhaps one impersonation (previous page) would have been left on the cutting room floor by today's producers. Orson Welles played his part too but experienced a fractious relationship with Sellers.

Lady Fiona McTarry a.k.a. Agent Mimi (Deborah Kerr) assists Sir James Bond (David Niven) to shoot down a barrage of explosive ducks with the exploding buttons she had sown on his jacket to kill him. Right: Woody Allen as Sir James Bond's crazy nephew Jimmy Bond a.k.a. Dr. Noah and the 'brain' behind the chaotic mayhem.

Left: Production Designer Ken Adam poses with Bond producer Cubby Broccoli on the interior super tanker set created on the specially built '007 Stage' at Pinewood Studios for *The Spy Who Loved Me* (1977). Below: Ken Adam's design drawing for 'Atlantis', Bond villain Stromberg's underwater lair that rises from the seabed.

THE OSCAR WINNING DESIGNER
by Sir Ken Adam

"I worked for Cubby Broccoli before Bond on three films one of which was *The Trials Of Oscar Wilde* with Peter Finch. For this I received the first prize from Visconti at the film festival in Moscow in 1972. Cubby and Harry Saltzman were the producers.

They approached me for *Dr. No*. I read the first 100 pages then gave them to my wife Letizia who said "This is rubbish! You can't prostitute yourself". Well I said, Terence Young is a good director and Cubby has made some good pictures so let's see. As it was to be a low budget film, under a million dollars, I seem to recall they were willing to give me a piece of the action.

It was a straight 'who dunnit'. No gadgets, just the sets and great locations in Jamaica. The most important thing for me was that I was able to design the sets without anyone looking over my shoulder as they were all in Jamaica. I had one talk with Terence "Listen Ken, just give me the right entrances and exits for the artists and I leave the rest to you." I was full on enthusiasm. Remember this was the 60's and I felt that film design was too antiquated, using old tricks like wood paper walls instead of the real stuff. So I played around with real materials, copper, stainless steel, to give the sets a new look. I told all the heads of department at Pinewood to keep a lookout for any new materials on the market and to keep me informed. I had a great team of people around me, like Johnny Stears who was my first special effects advisor and then Derek Meddings. They were first class but both sadly died too early. Fantastic people.

On *Dr. No* I filled three stages at Pinewood and by the time Terence returned from Jamaica he was raving with excitement. On one particular set I was advised by two young scientists from Harvard for the water reactor in which *Dr. No* drowns. For the island where the

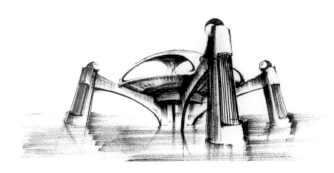

professor meets *Dr. No*, I devised a set on a platform almost in perspective, with a gigantic grill in the ceiling, a copper door and a table with a small case and with a Tarantula in it, nothing more!

On the *The Spy Who Loved Me* and *You Only Live Twice* the sets were the most challenging to design, the super tanker set and the huge volcano.

I pulled out all the stops! The crater for the volcano we built at Pinewood. After the filming the set was still standing leading to all sorts of complaints, that it was an eyesore, so we had to pull it down. To be sure not to make the same mistake again when I built an even bigger set I also built a stage around it and that became the 007 stage for *The Spy Who Loved Me*.

The budgets for the Bond sets increased with each picture. For *You Only Live Twice* it was a million dollars. I didn't go much over that but it was a tremendous responsibility for my team.

When scouting for locations I would film everything on my 16 millimetre Bolex, sometimes even from the

Above: Ken Adam's concept sketch of Blofeld's volcano lair built (right) for *You Only Live Twice* (1967) at Pinewood Studios. "The volcanoes in Japan stimulated me. When I came back to Pinewood I started scribbling." The set towered 126 feet above the Pinewood backlot and used two hundred miles of tubular steel.

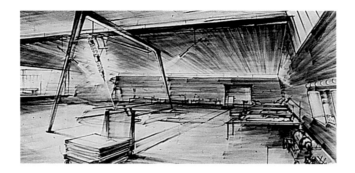

air. On *ThunderBall* we used a villa in Nassau for its two pools that we filled with seawater and sharks. The villa belonged to a wealthy couple called the Sullivans who liked a drink come nightfall. I was so scared Mrs Sullivan would fall in!

In the pool I constructed a corridor made of plexiglass sheets so Sean could swim on one side separated from the sharks. But I couldn't get enough 10 x 8 sheets, even sent a plane to Miami, but nothing… So I had a guard in the water as a precaution. Either the guard did not see or wasn't paying attention but a shark got past him and went straight for Sean. We shouted "get out!" and you've never seen Sean move so quickly. That could have been disastrous.

In those days there was no CGI so everything was done for real and we never wanted to cheat or fool the audience. In *ThunderBall* the flying machine that Bond straps on to his body came from the US army. You could only fly for about three minutes but still it worked. Again, no trickery. When you are experimenting with the biggest sets ever built, flying helicopters into enclosed areas, shooting off cliffs, you go through a lot of anxiety, but when all these things work that is when you are happy.

I fulfilled two ambitions in my life for I never knew if I wanted to be a theatrical or a film designer. I therefore combined the two because I used stylized theatrical design for films. In order to be a good film designer one has to be prepared to not just imitate reality but invent a form of reality that is acceptable to the audience. What was so satisfying to me was that I achieved this. In *Goldfinger* for instance, the set for the Fort Knox interior I built in gold which of course does not exist. After the film's release, United Artists received over 300 letters asking how was a British film unit allowed access to Fort Knox when even the President is not! They believed it! In *Dr. Strangelove* the War Room set was purely my imagination, I was not imitating reality. The true story behind that film was that when Reagan became President he asked his Chief of Staff if he could see the War Room. To which the reply was "Mr President, we do not have a War Room" ∎

Left: Ken Adam's production sketch for the laser table set in *Goldfinger* (1964). Above Ken designed a 'cathedral of gold' to depict the imagined interior of Fort Knox, something not even the President of the United States is allowed to visit. Right: Oddjob (Harold Sakata) races down the stairs into the gold vault to grapple with James Bond (Sean Connery).

Pages 6-7

Pages 8-9

Pages 10-11

Pages 12-13

Pages 14-15

Pages 16-17

Pages 18-19

Pages 20-21

Pages 22-23

Pages 24-25

Pages 26-27

Pages 28-29

Pages 30-31

Pages 32-33

Pages 34-35

Pages 36-37

Pages 38-39

Pages 40-41

Pages 42-43

Pages 44-45

Pages 46-47

Pages 48-49

Pages 50-51

Pages 52-53

Pages 54-55

Pages 56-57

Pages 58-59

Pages 60-61

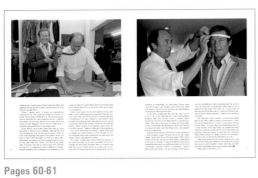

Pages 62-63

Pages 64-65

Pages 66-67

THE GIRLS:
JILL MASTERSON
by Shirley Eaton

Pages 68-69

Pages 70-71

Pages 72-73

Pages 74-75

Pages 76-77

Pages 78-79

Pages 80-81

Pages 82-83

THE ENGLISH GIRL
by Joanna Lumley

Pages 84-85

Pages 86-87

Pages 88-89

Pages 90-91

MISS CARUSO
by Madeline Smith

Pages 92-93

Pages 94-95

Pages 96-97

Pages 98-99

Pages 100-101

Pages 102-103

Pages 104-105

Pages 106-107

Pages 108-109

Pages 110-111

Pages 112-113

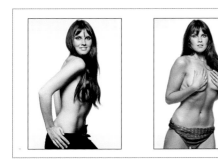

Pages 114-115

Pages 116-117

Pages 118-119

Pages 120-121

Pages 122-123

Pages 124-125

Pages 126-127

Pages 128-129

Pages 130-131

Pages 132-133

Pages 134-135

Pages 136-137

Pages 138-139

Pages 140-141

Pages 142-143

Pages 144-145

Pages 146-147

Pages 148-149

Pages 150-151

Pages 152-153

Pages 154-155

Pages 156-157

Pages 158-159

Pages 160-161

Pages 162-163

Pages 164-165

Pages 166-167

Pages 168-169

Pages 170-171

Pages 172-173

Pages 174-175

Pages 176-177

Pages 178-179

Pages 180-181

Pages 182-183

Pages 184-185

ALL ABOUT BOND

Photographs by Terry O'Neill
Edited by Deborah Moore and Robin Morgan